My Source of Strength

Norma Arce

Printed in USA

Glorified Publishing
PO Box 8004
The Woodlands TX 7738

DEDICATION

This book is first dedicated to my God, whom without Him, I would have been lost with no hope and no future.

My gratitude to my husband and my two sons. I thank God for them, for they have been such an inspiration to me.

Also my parents, who taught me unconditional love for God, and are in heaven enjoying His holiness.

CONTENTS

INTRODUCTION

I am obeying what the Lord put in my heart. He said to me one day, "Write down everything that I have done and said to you and your family." So I obeyed. I started writing all my experiences with God down in a blank notebook. The more I wrote, the more friends just kept on giving me blank notebooks as gifts, without them even knowing. Every time I would finish one, I would get another blank notebook. I thought to myself, "What a coincidence is this?"

I kept writing my experiences down in books. It wasn't until one day the Lord put in my heart, "Write a book." I thought, "Nah! I am just imagining this." Then I heard it again. I ignored it two, or maybe three, times. Then a friend of my husband's, who was an awesome man of God, came over the house one day for dinner. He said to me, "Why haven't you written the book?" I just looked at my husband, puzzled and excited.

How many times has that happened to you? For you see, God knows everything! He will tell you things, and if you need just a little bit more understanding, or a couple of reminders, he will send someone else to tell you more clearly. I understood at that point what God was trying to tell me. At first I doubted it, so he sent a messenger to remind me of my assignment, and what I had to do. Because of His obedience, it is with much excitement and sincerity that I can say, here it is – my first book!

This is a book about hope for everyone. It's about miracles, and how God has not changed. Hebrews 13:8 says, *"Jesus Christ is the same yesterday, today, and forever."*

.

1 CHAPTER ONE

I would like to start by telling you a little bit of my testimony; how my encounter with that awesome God has totally changed my life, and also by saying, "God is good, all the time!" This has become a very important saying for me. It has become my total existence. I never knew God was good all the time, until I lived it.

I was born in the year 1957. Although my mother said she doesn't quite remember the events of how the things that happened to me happened, personally I think she would rather not say, or remember. The Lord has healed her pain in a very special way. She did, however, tell me a few of the things that happened. This is how I came to know about my childhood.

Personally it helped me to understand later, when I was older, why I was in such a mess. I had to deal with myself very carefully. I learned to like, and love myself so much more than I used to. You have to understand something: you yourself have to take charge of your life. No one else can do that for you. I cannot decide for you what path to take; you have to choose for yourself.

God has always been looking for a personal relationship with us. It's up to you as an individual to allow it to happen. My life is totally different than yours. You must do it for yourself, and make your own decision. "For you, and only you my Lord, healed my sick body and gave me a new heart!" He is my healer and my source of strength.

I was born in Puerto Rico in a town called Aguadilla. I was a normal healthy baby girl according to what my mother told me. My mother married my father at the age of eighteen. My father was a little bit older than her, not by much. My mother was the oldest of thirteen children. She only studied up to the third grade of elementary school, can you imagine that? Her father, my grandfather, took her out of school to help her mother, my grandmother, raise her brothers and sisters.

My mother told me that this broke her heart because she loved school. This may sound sad and it was, but this was a normal thing in the days when my mother was growing up as a little girl. My mother helped raised all of her brothers and sisters. I'm sure it was very hard for her as a little girl with so many chores to do. You can see now why she doesn't like to speak about her younger years.

When she was seventeen years old she met my father. My father was a local neighborhood boy. He was very good looking. I saw a couple of pictures of him. He was thin with black hair and his skin was caramel in color. He was a very handsome man, and I'm not just saying this because he was my father. He grew up about one mile away from my mother's house. They knew each other since they were both very young. I don't know much about their relationship because, as I mentioned earlier, my mother doesn't speak much about any part of her young life. My parents got married and became Christian, following God.

When my parents got married they had four children right away. We are a year apart. I have two older brothers and a younger sister. I am sort of the middle child who was always sick, for reasons that I will explain later. My parents, especially my dad, traveled a lot to New York City. His job took him back and forth between there and Puerto Rico. You see, my father was a truck driver during the sugar cane season in Puerto Rico. That was only for about six months out of the year. He was a private car service driver, and the rest of the time he was without work. He did not make much money doing this type of work in Puerto Rico, and he had to feed four kids plus my mother, the utilities and whatever other medical bills came along. That didn't include the normal bills that everyone else has. Oh, Lord, how we all can relate to that.

My mother was pregnant with me in her belly when my father said he was going to go to New York and stay there for a while to work. This is what my mother told me. While he was in New York City, he knew that there he would find work right away, and he did. That was so easy for him to find work that he decided to go live in New York City. There he would work and send my mother money for all of us. I guess that must have been really hard for my mother and my father, that decision to be left by herself, raising my two brothers.

My grandfather did not approve of any of their plans. He was totally against this, because part of that plan was my mother had to move in with her parents for a while until my father came back. At that point, no one knew when that would be. My mother was pregnant, had no money, could not work and had two other kids. She had no other choice but to move in with her parents.

My mom was pregnant and needed so much help. Part of that was the reason she moved with my grandparents. When I was born, my father was living in New York with his mother. I did not see my father until I was already ten months old. All I knew was my mom. My mother tells me when I first met my father I did not want him. He was a stranger. I was glad she said this to me, because it explained so much in my life! It took a while for me to be close to my dad, to so much as give him a smile. It took a couple of months of my father trying real hard to make friends with me for me to get a little closer to him.

Deep in my heart, this was real hard for me, because as I grew up I could remember and I always felt so far away from my father. I did not have confidence, nor did I feel like I could talk to him about my feelings. It was as if we had this distance from each other, and I could never quite explain why. I love my father very much, but yet we were not very close. We were distant. Something was definitely missing for him and me.

My sister was born a year later. At that time my father was home from New York City for reasons that I can't remember, and he was back in Puerto Rico to stay. My father bought the property across the street from my mother's parents, and he also bought a wooden house from a relative of his. He and my mother's brothers put the house together. It was great! We had a home. We were all together having so much fun.

My younger sister, who was a baby, got all the attention from my dad, and because she was younger they were very close. She was his little girl, and I was not. I always felt so left out of that relationship. But you know what? To me this was all right, or so I thought at that time. I always said to myself, "Oh, well! I have my mom. I don't need him." I thought my sister was so privileged that she had a dad and a mom, but as always, I accepted the situation that I was living, and kept on with my life.

I realized, as I got older in years, that my sister had a lot to deal with also by not having Mom. My sister and I had all that emotional loneliness and bitterness to deal with. I knew that God would help her, just like He helped me, and was always there comforting me. We were often left alone because my parents were always working, or far away in New York City. All we had was each other, all four of us, during our early childhood years.

I guess life was good, as good as I could remember. As a child we do not know what adult parents go through. Then, things started getting bad again. My parents, well my dad, lost his job again. They both started leaving to New York together, and leaving us with my grandparents. Sometimes when my parents would leave it would hurt, but I learned to deal with it by just shutting it out of my life a day at a time. I have to tell you, that to shut things out is not good for anyone. This causes bitter roots to settle in your heart, one on top of another, until it is extremely difficult to remove them. We create such pain piled up inside of us, that only the Grace of God can heal us from it.

Believe me when I tell you that these bitter roots have to come out. The only way that I know, that worked for me, was to bring them to the altar to Jesus as a sacrifice. He died on the cross for our afflictions and He took every pain for you and me. His blood was shed for us. Trust in Him. Just give Him all your hurt and you will see that Jesus will heal your heart in such a wonderful and peaceful way. He knows your sorrow and He will heal you totally. *"He lifted the needy out of their afflictions"* (Psalm 107:41). Listen to the word of God! It is still alive.

The way life is, you would think it's so complicated, yet at the same time so simple. You have to understand that life is hard when you don't serve God. When you are with God, and try to serve Him, it's no picnic either, because the enemy comes at you full force. However, I can't imagine life without

God, not having any hope. But we must remember one important thing: with God there is peace that surpasses all understanding! With this peace you can deal with anything that may come your way, in a totally different way. *"Peace I leave with you; my peace I give you"* (John 14:27). Without God you do not have this peace, so things are much, much harder.

I grew up in a Christian home. We went to church every Sunday. We did everything in church: we sang, praised, and we were active members of the church. We thought we were doing everything right, yet there was no spiritual growth. When my sister was born, my parents decided to move to New York permanently. Oh, how hard that was for me, leaving friends behind and moving to a far away place. It was in the month of December; I remember the snow. That was such a beautiful sight to see, and yet eerie, all at once.

My parents loved Puerto Rico. They had been there all their lives. Leaving Puerto Rico was leaving our only home, the home we came to love. I was around nine years old. My mother told me these stories of how I was sick all the time. I guess part of it was the changes in the climate from hot to cold, and not really understanding the huge cultural change for a kid at that time. It was a huge change for my mother as well. It was hard. We moved to New York in the midst of winter. That was a huge change for us in many ways imaginable.

I hated all of it, the weather, the apartment, and the schools. We went from playing outside in a warm place, a carefree life, to being locked up all day, watching television with nothing else to do. It was too cold.

I would always think and remember the small, wood house in Puerto Rico. I remember we had no bathroom. We used to take showers in the kitchen in a bucket. There was a small curtain dividing the kitchen from the rest of the little house. I remember playing house underneath the house. My dad had chickens under there, and we used that as a house. It was so much fun.

I told my sons some of these stories. They thought that I was prehistoric, and very poor. I knew this by something they had said. They looked very sad and said, "Mom, you are so old, and you were so poor?" I just laughed! Imagine no toilet and no shower. They thought, "Wow! This lady is real old!" At the same time they reacted, my little one at one point said, "I'm sorry, Mom. You must have gone through so much when you were a little girl." That touched my heart! It was overwhelming, and I just cried.

Well, we had our little wooden house, and it was great I thought. You have to understand, this was a kid who thought everything was great as long as we were all together. That is how our heart should be in front of the Lord: a heart of a child. No matter what is happening around us; no matter how mean people are, and even if they treat you harsh, our hearts should be like a child. Children see no wrong, no worry, no pain, have no hate or care in the world. Children forget about any hard time around them, and anyone who hurts them. At that time, this was me - no worries, not a care in the world, other than the fact that I was always sick, and had very little strength left to play or do much. Well I really do not know what happened after that because I cannot remember much of it, and my mother does not want to talk about those days. They were painful to her, she said.

The first time we went to New York, I was around three or four. My mother does not want to speak about this time either; she is totally in denial about this. I don't know why. I hope some day she tells me. I feel that it will help her emotional state, and help me to better understand what happened to me, and why. I also feel she can be healed of so much hurt and suffering within her life and her heart.

According to Mom, I came back home from New York sick and I kept getting worse. I would not eat a thing. My mother did not know what to do. She took me to a doctor in Puerto Rico, a pediatrician. As a matter of fact I went back to Puerto Rico when I was married. I saw my old doctor and was able to introduce him to my family. What a nice surprise he was still alive, and he was so happy to see me. It was just great! He told my husband I was a miracle.

Back to the story, as I was told: because of my lack of appetite and not eating, I became very ill. I had very poor nutrition. I was anemic and had other complications that, if I were to talk about them, would take pages and pages to mention. I could not walk. I had lost all my strength and the ability to move my legs, so I did not walk much. I still don't understand, really, what was wrong with me. My mother said she had no clue of what was going on. She kept me home, tried as best as she could to just feed me, but I would not eat. I would spit it out if I ate anything. My father just prayed, which was hard, because they were not such strong believers. My dad did, I guess, the best he could. "Lord, let it be your will in my daughter's life, please heal her". So my mother told me.

It must have been a hard time for my parents to see their little girl dying before their eyes, and the doctors couldn't do anything about it. My stomach was shutting down, and I was in severe pain all the time. They had no clue as to why I was dying before their eyes, and what caused all this. The last thing the doctors said was, "There is nothing else we can medically do. There is no hope for her. Take her home." My father told me that he put my crib by the window. I was just five years old. My father thought, "I will put her little bed by the window so that the sun can shine on her when she goes to heaven." Really, he was accepting and going by what the doctors had said.

The doctors had sent me home to die. They told my father that I was not going to get any better, and I was not going to make it through the day, so it was just a matter of time.

My father told me that my mom and him just waited and watched me. As they waited, watching me, all of a sudden the black pupils of my eyes started to move up and up and up, and I was gone. All my father saw was the white of my eyes. My father panicked and he cried out, "She is dying!" My father screamed in fear. Amazingly, on the street where my mother lived, up the road there was a huge building, white in color. This was a Pentecostal church that my parents attended from time to time, praise God.

My father ran up the road searching for hope, and he found it. He got the pastor, explained quickly the urgency, and they both ran down the road to where I was, with no life in me, in the small crib. My father said to the pastor, "Help my daughter!"

How many of you know that there is power in the name of Jesus, to heal the sick and to perform miracles? The pastor started praying for life, praying for a miracle, so that the Lord would be glorified! *"To God be the honor and glory for ever and ever"* (1 Timothy 1:17). I guess you know what happened, since I am writing this book! Yes, I was brought back to my parents, glory to God!

I have a picture of this event in my possession. My mom gave it to me, because a few Sundays passed, and when I was better, I was brought to church to show the congregation God's awesome miracles, so that God would be glorified. After that I was partially paralyzed. I couldn't walk for a while due to the lack of body fluids in me, which caused lack of fluid in my knees. Of course, the Lord healed me from that, also! Again, He is a

God of miracles!

2 CHAPTER TWO

My father had more financial hardship, so he sold the wooden house. He lost his job, so he had to leave again, back to New York City. Here we were, four of us and my mother, living in my grandfather's house again. Neither my grandfather nor my grandmother wanted us living with them again, and again. They just did not like us living there; it was too much to help us. I never understood my grandparents. Why didn't they love us? Why did they not want us living there? They had a big house, with two levels, that was partially empty. My grandfather was always telling my mother spiteful things, like how my father was irresponsible and always broke, among other things. I know that during these trying times it was real hard for my mother, also. Around a year after my father left to New York, my mother left with him. He sent for her so that they could both work, and earn more quickly the money they needed to get us.

There we were - my two older brothers, me and my younger sister, left alone with my grandparents who did not want us there. I was so heartbroken at both my parents and grandparents. It is so horrible for a kid not to feel wanted or loved. I was about ten years old and I remember how awful I felt every day. I went to school, came home, and I had a lot of chores to do after school - no playing, no fun or games. My grandfather would not have it any other way. It was such a hard life for a young child to have.

You just cannot imagine how hard my chores were, especially since I had no idea of what I was doing. One of the many things I had to do was walk about a mile to a river to get two buckets of water for my grandmother. This was every day when I came from school. The buckets were so heavy. Every day that went by, I became bitter. I just was so angry, and so lonely that I welcomed the hard chores. You just accept life. What else could I do, tell my parents?

All this was so difficult for me to understand as to why was this happening. I felt it was only to us, and no one else. I had cousins that, no matter what they were going through, they were home with their mom and dad; yet, we had to go through these abandonment issues and live with people who hated us. For this reason, and for all my other circumstances and abandonment, I became an extremely bitter and rebellious child. I never smiled, and was consumed with negative thoughts. I was so lonely, and battling such anger inside; yet, I was always singing! In the songs I would try to drown all of my hurt. I loved to sing. It made me forget all of my troubles. I now know that the Bible says, *"For what is our hope, or joy, or crown of rejoicing? It is not even you in the presence of our Lord Jesus Christ at His coming?"* (1 Thessalonians 2:19).

During that period of my childhood, while we were alone in Puerto Rico, my mom would come to visit us during Christmas and bring us presents. I hated my parents for that and I hated the gifts. I would not play with any of them. I never told my mother anything of how and what I was feeling. I just kept it inside, where no one knew. To this day I still have a brand new doll that she brought me from New York, one of those Christmases that they came to see us. I have never used it. I don't even look at it. It's just a reminder of a difficult and painful time. I find it hard to explain to a person when they ask me about the doll in the box. I just thank God that I prayed to Him all the time! I would cry out, "Lord please help me never to leave you, ever." *"God is our refuge and strength"* (Psalm 46:1).

I knew that through His mercy he would help me, and He never left me. *"I will never leave you nor forsake you"* (Joshua 1:5). Now I know that he has always been there for me, no matter what. I thank God for His friendship, His love, and most of all, His mercy. *"They are new every morning"* (Lamentations 3:23).

After two years, my mother came from New York to get us. I was around eleven or twelve. We stayed in New York, and we grew up there, and I became a very strong willed teenager. I still went to church and loved God. The most amazing thing would happen to me, that no matter what church I went to, the Lord always had a prophetic word for me! This was so great, as I became so used to hearing from God in one way or another! Every time that I would go to church, God would always call me out and speak to me. I truly know that God knew all my hurt, and all that needed to be dealt with in my life. Thank God that part of my life has not changed; He still is the same as always.

God is the only one that was faithful to me, and has never changed. He has always been there for me. Although I grew up knowing God and His word, I had not yet felt that special touch from the Father. Even though I knew who He was, I didn't really know Him. I knew He was love, compassion, and all that, but yet I felt like there had to be more to this. God is so awesome! He knows exactly when to let His presence be known and seen.

He always arrives on time; not a minute before or after, but always at the precise, exact moment.

I was raised up to be a good Christian girl. I learned all the stories of the Bible, the main characters of the Bible, and everything that you are taught about God, His Son and The Holy Spirit. I thought I knew God, but I didn't really know Him. I kept making one mistake after another. I was just such a rebellious child! I felt that I could do everything on my own without anyone's help. Most of the time I could not understand my own judgment calls, but I was determined with my own will and thoughts to try to get it right.

I got married when I was eighteen years old. I married a man who was not Christian, nor did he have any type of beliefs. My mother really liked him, but my father did not. We went to the same school and we lived on the same street, so we knew each other for a long time. As we got older, we got closer and started dating. This led to, let's get married - so we were engaged. This made my mom very happy! She started planning my wedding, and it was crazy.

Until one day, something happened. It was July 4th celebration. I remember it so well. It was raining. I saw my fiancée leaving in a cab with another woman, and they were all dressed up. At first I thought, "He would never do anything like that to me! It can't be him. That cannot be him, no way, but then I realized…Oh, wow! That's him!" After all, it was in front of his house. I felt so betrayed by him.

The more I thought about it, the more I realized he did me wrong. That night, I remember, it was raining and it was around 10:00 o'clock. I saw him getting out of a cab, and I ran out in the rain towards his house. I said to him, "How could you do this?" I gave him back the engagement ring.

He just gave me a chuckle side laugh. I was so angry! I knew he was up to no good.

When I told my mother what I had done, she was devastated. She told me, "Get the ring back!" She said, "You are planning a wedding! There are already too many things done, plus all the things that we have bought!" My mom spoke with him regarding what he did, and he said he was helping a friend out, that's all. I felt bad for my mom, all she had already gone through, and all her expenses.

He came back the following night to see me, and he asked me, what happened? We spoke. I told him I was hurt. I was mostly hurt because of my mom, so I put my feelings aside as usual. We agreed that he made a mistake and we then got married. I knew that it was a mistake to get married. It was too much to go back, so I got married.

Word of advice: Never, ever marry someone that you feel in your heart has done you wrong to please someone else - *no matter who it is*. It just doesn't work! Your heart is not in it, at least mine wasn't. I was only married one and a half years, and it was not pretty. Towards the end of my so-called marriage, my ex-husband got incredibly drunk one night. I prefer not to go into details because it hurts too much, but I got pregnant that night with my oldest son.

We already had big problems. Both of us were not getting along. We pretended, and acted as husband and wife for appearances. My parents and I loved God, so I hung in there, and I did try to work it out. We were both so young, and we both had a lot of problems, and we were almost at the brink of breaking up anyway. We both were making horrible mistakes.

While I was pregnant, there were terrible things I went through. I was always alone, sad and miserable. I became so sick, I guess from everything I was going through, all that emotional mess, that the doctors had to put me in the hospital. They made an emergency decision, and kept me there for three months in the ICU unit. My baby and I almost died. Several times Satan tried to end my life,and that of my son's, without succeeding.

We had to pray so much for my son, that the Lord would help him and me during this period of time while I was in the hospital. I felt it was just a strong war against my life, and my oldest son's life. My son's father was hardly ever around while I was pregnant or while I was in the hospital going through so much. He would come once in a while to see me, and he was not right. This created a lot of problems for me in the hospital. He would have arguments with the staff, and with the doctors. It was a difficult situation. All I had with me during this horrendous time was my father. I wanted nothing to do with this man, my son's father. I just wanted a divorce; he left me alone during a time in my life that I need him the most, just like that rainy night when he betrayed me. He left me alone then, too, for someone else.

My father stood with me through the pain and suffering of the hospital and all the other things that I went through. There was this one day, I got real bad, and my father could never find my ex-husband whenever an emergency arose. The doctors could not find him either, and because of this, my life was constantly at risk. We needed him for signatures on forms because of the gravity of my pregnancy, and he could not be found. It became necessary for my father to be given power of attorney over my life because someone had to sign legal papers. I was in a life and death situation.

How ironic life is, when I was little, dying, my father got a priest to pray for me and now during all this life and death, there's my father again, helping me pull out of death into life. I thank God so much for dad and I felt so different towards my father from that point on for all he did for me and for my son. My father saved my life in more ways than I could imagine; yes, one more time from death.

I remember one year I was in the hospital during the thanksgiving holiday and Christmas holiday. My father - or my Papi like I used to call him - came to the hospital to see me. I will never forget this day for as long as I live. It was raining real hard outside as I looked through the window, and it was so cold. My father snuck in the hospital after visiting hours and got caught. I felt so bad; he was bringing me Thanksgiving dinner. The doctors had me on a special, strict diet, so there was no way they were going to let me eat that yummy food. They told my father no! She cannot eat that food. I thought nooooooo!

Well, I started to cry, and cry uncontrollably! Number one, I was alone in a room for the holidays with tons of machinery attached to me. The medical staff had gone away and I was left with a few staff members; and, number two my dad had spent time home and cooked the turkey dinner for me. How sad! As I think back on this time, I want to cry!

My blood pressure shot sky high because of the crying. I was so upset that the doctors became concerned for my health and welfare. Finally, they said, "Ok, ok! She can have a little bit." Boy, talk about eating and gobbling it all up! There was turkey, and fresh fruits that dad had brought. Thank you, Daddy, for all you did for me by making that thanksgiving special for you, me, and BJ, your grandson. I will love you, Dad, always!

Finally, even through all that suffering, after three months, my miracle son was born in December. He was a very cute preemie, a very skinny, long, baby boy, only four ounces and twenty-one inches. A baby that doctors said would be deformed; that he did not look like a baby at all, but a thing - that's what the doctors said. Yes, God proved them all wrong.

I was so happy, even though he was on all kinds of machinery, because he was a preemie baby, and my miracle! He was truly a miracle from God. My son was on a respirator when he was born. His lungs were not fully developed. It was very difficult for me to come and see him, but I did, every day. I always thanked God for him.

Going back, when I think of what the doctors kept telling me about my son, they would say things like, "I should have an abortion", because he was going to be deformed and he was going to be born like a fish with his hands stuck together like webs and his feet as well. I hung in there believing and praying so much, I believed the Word of God for a miracle while I was sick in the hospital. I just kept on praying for a miracle and the Lord my God did it! My baby was born perfect because everything God gives you is perfect. Praise is to God who gives life, and takes life, and has a purpose in everything that happens.

I lived with my mother while my baby was in the hospital, and while I was recuperating. My father was happy to have me home and take care of me. Through this ordeal my mother was gone to Puerto Rico. I don't remember why, but now, I just find it strange that my mother would always disappear when I was going through things.

3 CHAPTER THREE

My son was one year old when I left his father. It took me such a long time for both my son and I to heal from this ordeal and I was trying to be strong for my son. His father was just getting worse and worse. He was drinking more frequently, coming home drunk, and was never around for me. I was always alone in my house with the baby. My father used to come to see me, and he felt so bad for me. My father would always say to me, "The doors of my house are always open for you and your baby." After many days of dealing with him drunk, and me feeling lonely, I became so hurt and bitter. I took the initiative and decided to leave him. It was just too much pain and hurt and abuse. I knew things between him and I had changed for the worse, and that we already had lost what little respect we had for each other.

I was always praying for God to open a door for me, if this was what He wanted, to help me leave him and move on. That did not happen for a while. One day, by chance, you might think, but, no! God does not work that way. Remember, I always fasted and prayed over my circumstances. The drinking, along with its lifestyle, changes things in a person's life. I was married to a man that did not love the Lord and resented me for it. That was my cross to bear.

I continued to pray and notice certain things in my life. For example, I was always totally left alone every night. Yes, that became his routine, but the difference was that we would not fight about it. To him, this lifestyle became ok, for him to do this night after night. I went out with my friends, and this was ok, also. I really, honestly, did not care what he did, or with whom he did it. Well, one day I came home from work early at lunchtime, and he was there. I knew something was different, and in my spirit something felt different. I asked him what he was doing home so early. He said he had an appointment. I left it alone, but I knew in my spirit something else had happened! Later on, I found out he was having an affair. I was not trying to find this out, nor was I looking, or watching him. It was sort of dropped in my lap, so I walked out and left him. I will share in a bit how this came about.

When I found out about his affair, he turned so violent. After this, he just drank way too much, and it was an incredibly ugly situation. He started accusing me of having affairs left and right. He accused me of being with his friends. I understood that I had to get out of this situation, and fast. Somehow, I knew this was going to end ugly. This was not a marriage. I was so lonely and hurt all the time. I had spoken to him about God, and he had refused. He did not want to go to church at all. I tried to get counseling for us, but he rejected it. He just said no to everything I would suggest.

I know I had a lot to be blamed for, but I don't think that I deserved what I got. I will tell you a little of what happened. I knew that I should not have married him, but it was too late to turn back. I started to pray for the Lord to help me, to please open a door for me if this life I was living was not his will. Remember, I thought that I was not loved, or cared for, by anyone. I was a completely lonely, unhappy woman, and so afraid for my life because of my husband and his drinking.

I prayed for the Lord to guide me. This went on for a few months. As I prayed, a thought came into my head -- to go back to school and better myself, because I knew that I was going to be alone and needed a better job. I signed up for school, and started studying. My new life was my school and back home every day, over and over, and this was ok, because I had a goal to reach: a better life for my son and me. I was still married, and it was ok, too, because I had a goal. During that time things were calm.

Then, one day, my aunt and my cousin came to visit. My aunt told me the truth, and what was really going on. They told me, "Keep an eye on your husband." I found that strange, so I asked her, what do you mean? She would not tell me. I started to keep a close eye on things, and one day I followed him. I needed to know! I was growing so weary from so much emotional drain, plus school, and I needed a way out.

Guess what? It was true! He had someone else. There he was, in the arms of another woman! She had long hair and looked average. At first, I thought, "Oh, wow! What now?" But it just did not bother me like I thought it would. I did not feel any hurt, or mistrust, or pain...nothing but relief. It was so strange what I was feeling! God truly was working with me. The only thing that I remember was, I felt such a sense of peace and relief at that moment, I started thanking God!

It may sound strange to you but you have to remember, I was praying constantly for God to either give me a way out, or for a complete change in my ex-husband. I was expecting one of the two, the change, or the way out, whatever God wanted for me. I felt as if it was an open door. The Bible does say, "Do not commit adultery," in Exodus 20:14, Deut. 5:18, Mark 10:19, and a lot more. The Bible also says if a husband or wife commits adultery, you have every right to leave him or her. Matthew 19:8 says, *"Moses permitted you to divorce your wives, but from the beginning it was not so."* It is lawful for a man to divorce his wife depending on the circumstances.

For many reasons which you have read, and a lot that I did not mention, I fell out of love with my ex-husband. I know now that part of it was I was angry with myself, and needed much healing. I had a lot of hatred, and bitterness, in me that God needed to work out. I knew that a heart like that could never hear the words of God, because my heart was hardened. My ex-husband always left me alone in the year and a half we were together. He was never really with me, and was never there for me. He was confused. He confessed to me some horrible things that he had done and was ashamed of, and asked me to forgive him. I asked him why, and he told me the reason he did what he did. It was just too ugly to even write. I pray that he gives his life to God. I know that the Lord will forgive him if he calls out to Him. You see, he has heard the Lord's Word and I know there has been a seed planted in his heart.

I left him and moved in with my aunt. My ex-husband became very violent. He was totally transformed into something so evil, he was no longer a calm person, but was now an angry, hateful person. I couldn't even stay in my home. I had to hide for a while. He always kept following me, and wherever he found me, he would yell at me, and sometimes hit me.

It got so bad for me. One time I will never forget he tried to rape me. His excuse was if I were pregnant with another child, I would have no place to go, and would have to move in with him! I know that angels of God were watching over me, and protected me, and no harm came to my son, or to me. I had to get a court order so he would leave me alone. My parents lived in Puerto Rico so I had no one else. My aunt was alright, and very kind, but it was not an easy situation. I started blaming myself, the fact that I saw him with another woman. I started to go through changes. I felt like I was dumb, and even ugly, and unwanted. After I moved in with my aunt, and she told me all of the ugly things that she found out and knew about him, my way of thinking changed. Then I knew better than to blame myself and doubt.

Time went by, and I healed a little bit from all that craziness. It was very hard. My father used to tell me, "You are young." My self-esteem was so low. I thought I was just so ugly that no one else would ever want me. My friends tried to set me up with dates, but I was so afraid of losing my son that I would turn them down. I went nowhere.

By now I was angry at the world, and at myself, for being so dumb. I would cry out late at night, "God, what do I do?" That was always my cry, and prayer, and my tears…so many tears. I thought everything was over; my life, my youth, yet I was only twenty-one. My ex-husband never left me alone. He was constantly harassing my son and me, and he was such a strain on my life. You just could not imagine, unless you are at this point or have at some point experienced something like this. I was so cornered by him that I knew I had to move on, and get him out of my life, once and for all. He hurt me too much. I moved away where he could not find me, at least for a while anyway. I was trying to buy myself some time.

After much crying, and much prayer, asking God to choose for me, I met someone. He was a guardian angel that I fell in love with. He was a wonderful man. He was so kind, gentle, and most important, understanding. He had such a giving heart. That was my attraction to him. I know that the Lord put him in my path to help me. He never questioned me. He just knew and understood I was so mixed up in my head about life and people and relationships. I was really stressed out.

We did not have time to date much because of my ex-husband and all the problems. He knew my mess because I told him, and he also saw many times the craziness of it all. We got married and have a wonderful son. I love my husband. I know that God gave him to me. There is no other explanation for his compassion, his understanding of me. I have suffered too much in my lifetime! I doubt that anyone else would have understood how I was, unless God had intervened.

I was a very difficult person to love. You see, I was never taught love; not by my mother nor by my father. Neither one of my parents ever hugged me or so much as gave me a kiss or ever said, "I love you!" while I was growing up. If they did, I truly do not remember. Once in a while my mom would hug me, not for long, just a tap or two. This is why I had no idea how to behave, what to say, or do, when it came to love. I thank God because my husband had enough love in him for the both of us put together! Without that I would have been lost. My husband is so kind, and so sweet. I named him *sweetheart;* that is all I call him! I told him a long time ago, "I call you sweetheart because you are so sweet, understanding and kind." That's my sweetheart.

The two of us have been through so much. I experienced a lot of pain as I grew stronger and was being healed by God. I knew the word of God; I also knew that a divorce was a hard thing. I always pray that every move in my life be given to me with the blessings from above. I had a problem for a while trying to get my mind and my thoughts in order. Remember, I had just been through a lot in my personal and spiritual life. I was always praying, "Lord, my father, please help me to understand what I cannot understand. This new man that I married, Lord, was he given to me by you or was it me?" I cannot believe the way the enemy will always bring doubt into your mind. How can I rectify the wrong that I did in my life, if all I do is keep making one mistake after another? "Please, Lord! Help me to understand all of this that has happened in my life!"

Well, I never stopped praying the same prayer. It had become part of me. I guess I knew the Lord would answer me one day. I will never forget when I went to a conference in Tampa, Florida. The conference was for women; one of the conferences was going to be for divorced women. I tell you this: my heart goes out to all divorced women. Believe it or not, when it comes to serving God, we are still in the old days when women were condemned because a man would divorce her for no reason. Women are still being persecuted, because there are some churches that will not let a divorced person have a ministry, or any part in the church. God forgives you of all your sins, but man can't. Well, in this conference, the divorce class was really good, and he spoke to us out of the Bible.

I remember as he finished the class, he stepped down from the pulpit. My pastor's wife was with me. The conference speaker was teaching us with two colored pieces of paper, one pink representing female and one green representing male. He took the two pieces of paper, taped them together, and then took them apart representing divorce by means of adultery. He went on, and spoke about a second marriage. Those two pieces of paper he glued together, representing God as the glue that keeps marriages together. You had to be there to understand how this man explained divorce. After this was all over, he finished and prayed. This man stepped down from the pulpit and came by where I was sitting. I was surprised when he said, "I have to pray for you. The Lord asked me to pray for you, and to tell you, that He united your marriage." He took the pieces of paper, pink and green, and gave them to me. He said, "God said, 'Like these two pieces of paper, He glued your marriage.'"

I was so touched because this was what I was praying for - an answer from God about my marriage. This man was used by the Holy Spirit to deliver this message to me in front of witnesses. After this happened, his wife came to us and said, "You women are blessed." In surprise, we asked, "Why?" She said, "My husband never lays hands on anyone. That's just the way he is, and he steeped down from the pulpit to lay hands on you. Truly that was from God." Oh, Lord! I can't believe all these years, and all that we have been going through, my husband and me, waiting for an answer… and here it was, finally!

The enemy has tried so hard to break us up; yet, putting the Lord first, and the love He has given us, keeps us together. It has been a lot of trials, and tribulations, but yet still we are there for each other. I thank God that there are still men out there that love the Lord and are devoted husbands and fathers. My husband is a father to our son, and he was a father to my oldest son. He loved my oldest son as if he was his own. He has always been there for him, and continuous to be there for him, now that my son lives on his own.

We brought our boys to church ever since they were little. The Bible does say *"Let the little children come to me, for theirs is the kingdom of heaven"* (Matthew 19:14). Just like me, I wanted them to have that Christian foundation. I wanted to plant a seed in them that will always be there, and grow with them as they grow. I have had one experience after the other with God. All of these experiences between these pages are for you to see, and understand, how powerful and great our Father is! Plus, we cannot forget merciful. I am sure I would have never finished these pages if I had kept on writing, and telling you about my life and my experiences with the Lord. I know that the most important thing in my life is God, and what he did back then, what He does now, and will keep doing - for you, the whole world and me.

4 CHAPTER FOUR

All this time and all those years I thought I knew God. I knew *about* God, but I had never truly, and really, had an encounter with Him and with the Holy Spirit. I used to ponder what people were always talking about, speaking in tongues and being blessed by the Holy Spirit. I read many times about it, and I patiently waited for that blessing to come to me one day.

We need to be less focused on our everyday issues, and more focused on Him, and His glory. *"And suddenly there came a sound from heaven, as of a rushing mighty wind, and it filled the whole house where they were sitting"* (Acts 2:2). I signed up for Bible Institute seminary. I studied about the Word, and God, and all there was to know, or so I thought; but yet, no speaking in other tongues and no blessing of the Holy Spirit. I was thinking, "What is wrong with me? And how come every one I know has it but me?"

I realized something. I prayed so hard for something that God wanted me to have, without truly knowing what I was asking. You see, the Holy Spirit is in you when you are born again. Speaking in tongues is a gift from above, as it is mentioned in the book of Acts. This is already in you! It was already in me! I was the one holding it back. I was the problem! Not God, nor the Holy Spirit.

I prayed every prayer imaginable, closed my eyes real tight and prayed, and waited. None of what I tried to do or how I asked would work. Yet, I went on faithfully and patiently, again waiting, and waiting, for His will to be done in my life. One Saturday evening in September, a lady preacher came to our church. We had a women's conference, and she was going to preach. She was an awesome preacher, had a wonderful personality and a powerful anointing from the Lord. She was preaching about the person of the Holy Spirit.

You must understand – Holy Spirit as a PERSON - that was an eye opener for me! I listened so closely to that preaching! I wanted to meet the person of the Holy Spirit. This caused a change in me. I was transformed into what seemed to be another world, another dimension! It was a great peace that I felt.

I closed my eyes and started to pray, thinking, "Wow! The Holy Spirit is a person that I can speak to!" While I was praying, the music continued playing this particular song, and the words went something like, "Holy Spirit, come and fill my life, fill my soul…" and when I closed my eyes and started to sing, "Fill me up, Holy Spirit, fill me up," something **happened!** It was like time stood still, and I was lost in the most beautiful, and peaceful, aroma. I was speaking in another tongue and it was so great! *"And they were all filled with the Holy Spirit and began to speak with other tongues, as the spirit gave them utterance"* (Acts 2: 4). I started thanking the Lord for my gift. Finally, I met the Holy Spirit! It was a great moment, a time that I would never forget, ever. Praise be to God! I love you, my father, my Lord.

This was just the beginning of God's plan in my life, and of all the wonderful things that He had planned for my family and me. After the blessing of other tongues, the Holy Spirit really came upon me. I kept growing and learning more about God, and His awesome anointing.

5 CHAPTER FIVE

I started getting closer to God. I started seeking and searching for Him more and more. I wanted to get to know God so much more intimately, that I started looking for Him more in a personal manner, just Him and I. By this I mean going to spiritual retreats, getting filled up in these retreats, separating myself with the Lord. In these retreats it was just me and God. This is what helped me and that is how I started. I told myself I needed more. I needed to know who God was, or at least I thought that I could figure him out. What a mistake! God is so massive that we can never figure him out! But, for me it was a good start. *"I am God almighty"* (Genesis 17:1).

As I sought to find more about God, I went to another women's retreat in March. It was so great! We need more of that power from all of us coming together in unity to worship Him (see Ephesians 4:13). I went with about fifteen women from our church. We all had wonderful experiences with the Lord. I will never forget how, at this retreat, the Lord spoke to me so clearly the second day that I was there. My oldest son was at that time sixteen years old. He wanted to leave home. He wanted to go and live with his father. I was totally against it, for many reasons. One of the reasons was his father was not Christian; he was still in the world, and I knew my son was at an age where he was looking for any type of so-called "fun".

There were other reasons why I did not want my son to go so far. My son was such a tool for sustaining me alive and in one place. He was the one that kept me from ending my life, many years ago, when I thought that it was all over for me. The devil played with my mind so much when I was alone that I used to look at my son, and my situation, and just cry. I knew that I could not leave that baby alone by himself. So that is why I fought so hard not to let him go. It might have been selfish of me, trying to keep my son. I guess you have to know all I went through to understand. When we do things outside of the will of God, or when we are disobedient, then everything just goes wrong.

I will never forget the experience I had while seeking more of God, and praying for my oldest son. I was praying quietly, "Lord Jesus help me," but this was a prayer of loneliness. I thought to myself, "I am going to pray in my mind." My thought process was that the devil couldn't hear it. Also, if I prayed out loud, then any one could hear my prayer, and I did not want anyone to know what I was going through.

You see, when you spend most of your life in the church as I did, you think you know everything. You find it extremely hard to believe people's prayers or prophecies, because you have seen so much. That is what I was going through. I did not want to hear from anybody but God. He could not tell me in my ear, because I would think it was just me thinking those thoughts. It couldn't come from my pastor, or anybody else, because I would start thinking he or she knew my situation. It had to be very personal, directly from God.

How many of you know that God is all knowing, all wise. He knows everything! "*For if our heart condemns us, God is greater than our heart, and knows all things"* (1 John 3:20). He knew all of my thoughts, even before I thought them!

I went into a room in this retreat by myself, because my stomach was hurting me so badly. I just wanted to be alone. The ladies that I came to the retreat with were going to do other things for a little while. I didn't want to do other things - I went there to look for God! I had no excuse to tell them, and they insisted that I go with them. I couldn't say no, after all, they had the car and they were my ride back and forth.

While we were in the store, all of a sudden, out of nowhere, my stomach started hurting me something awful. I said to them, "I can't go anywhere like this. Please take me back to the hotel, and then you can go wherever you want to go." That is exactly what they did. As I walked into the hotel, the minute that I stepped in the lobby door, instantly the pain in my stomach was gone! I thought about it and thanked Jesus for healing my pain. I walked through the lobby and came upon this room. In this room there were about ten women, some from my church and some from other churches. They were praying, praising God, and crying so hard. I went and joined them.

I say to you today, God's plans are not our plans! *"For I know the plans I have for you"* (Jeremiah 29:11). He has an agenda for our lives and we are the ones that sometimes mess it up. I know that it is hard, but we have to try to not help God! He does not need our help; He needs us to submit to His will. He knows what He is doing in our lives. I went into this room, and boy, what an eye opener! The Lord took a hold of me, and He actually gave me an audience! Let me explain. If you have never experienced an audience with the King it was great, awesome, and WOW! I was moved in my spirit! This is the only way that I could describe it. Just like Philip in

Acts chapter 7, *"Now when they came up out of the water, the Spirit of the Lord caught Philip away, so that the eunuch saw him no more; and he went on his way rejoicing."* This is in the New Testament, where the Bible says that the Holy Spirit took him and brought him to an Ethiopian.

I will try to explain, as best as I possibly can, how this experience was with the King. I was taken in my spirit to this big, awesome room. There, in this room, I felt a mighty presence. I could not see this presence, for I could not look up. I was in a kneeling position, bowing down my head. There were two, really long steps. The floor color was like an onyx, pearl, silvery antique color, and a color that I have never seen or can barely explain to you at this point. I was dressed all in white from head to toe. You could not see my hair, for it was all covered up. It was like a nun's outfit, beautiful long and white.

I was there and I never spoke through my mouth. It was communication through thoughts. It was so great! This big presence stood up, and said to me, "You wanted to ask me something, and you wanted me to answer. Well, here I am." Oh, wow! I started to speak, however, you must remember it was through my thoughts. I continued to communicate this way, telling this awesome Person about my son. I understood what was going on, and what I was saying. I started to say how my son was mine and how he could not leave me, and how my heart was totally broken because of this. The presence in that room stood up and said to me, "Be still." He then asked me, "Who am I?" Then He asked me again, "Who am I?" I stopped, and said, "Jehovah." He said, "I gave him to you, and I can take him from you. Let him go, and give him to me." When I heard that, I cried, and bowed down my head in His presence. Then, instantly, I was back in the prayer room with the other women.

The ladies in that room said to me, "Where were you all this time?" I was just speechless for a long time as I lay on the floor. My friend Patty told me that all that time I was speaking in tongues. She said I kept making hand movements, and gestures, and I was having a very interesting conversation with God. I was making cradle movements as if I was rocking a baby. She said they knew I was praying for one of my kids, and they recognized the word Jehovah in tongues. All of them were there, and were witnesses of what happened to me. I thank God that all this happened in this prayer room, because if they had not been there, I would have thought it was all a dream.

In that retreat I experienced a lot of new and wonderful things. It was three o'clock in the morning, and all the ladies that went to the retreat were still in the presence of God. There was a lady there that the Lord was using so powerfully to minister to us. She was teaching us about the anointing of God upon us. That was one of the things that has always fascinated me, how is this possible? When you are so curious about God, and who He is, he will make a way for you to get to know Him more.

I was listening really carefully to everything that she was saying. It was so intense to hear about all the gifts that our father has for his children. Around one o'clock in the morning, we were all sitting on the floor listening to her wisdom of God. She leaned over to me and said, "The Lord wants to give you something…a gift," and she started speaking in tongues. It was beautiful the way she spoke! It was like she was communicating between her and God, or her spirit and God. I said, "Wow! That is so beautiful. I would love that!" I started asking, "What is that? I love it!"

God showed her my thoughts right at that moment! She said, "The Lord wants you to have that gift."

I was so overwhelmed. All through the night, she started teaching me the spiritual giftings, and how that world was...the beauty of God the Father, the Son and the Holy Spirit. I learned so much that night and I went back home so full of the knowledge and anointing of God. It wasn't until that Sunday night service that I knew that I had that gift, that ability to speak through my spirit to another person's spirit. It was a great feeling.

My husband was next to me, and the church was praising God in an awesome worship song. I leaned over to my husband and started to speak in tongues, but it was so different - it was a new tongue language. My spirit was talking with my husband's spirit! When it was over he said he felt such a peace inside him. The glory and honor belongs to my Lord. He also said that while I was speaking in tongues to him, there was silence all around him. He heard nothing but my voice. Let me remind you that the church was praising, and singing out loud. I thank God that I remember every detail of that event! It is so fresh in my mind, as if this was yesterday. All the glory and the honor are to the Father, the Son, and The Holy Spirit. Amen.

That entire three days experience was so wonderful. I knew God just a little bit more. But that was not enough for me! I wanted much more. I love the way that anointing felt, being in that presence. It was great! There was such joy, yet at the same time, such peace, and gladness all around me. I never wanted to get away from that natural spiritual high! I still wanted more.

One time I went to a church to speak about a children's ministry program. After I spoke, I returned back to my church. That night my pastor preached about Elijah, and the double portion. He was blessing, and praying for everyone. There was a long line and I got in it. When it was my turn to have hands laid on me, the Lord started speaking to me through the pastor. He said, "I gave you such an anointing in your hands, because your ministry is big. I give you the gift of discernment! I will show you people's problems - what they are dealing with and going through - so that you pray for them." I love you Jesus, so much, for all that You have given me! The more I seek You, the more I find You.

I love to speak of the wonders of God, and what He would do for you, if you just let Him work in your life. As you continue in your day-to-day life with the Lord, I want you to remember our Father, who is in heaven, wants to give us so much - if we let Him. On my birthday, my husband, my sweetheart, who is so sweet, bought me a brand new car. Again, here is my Lord giving me the little desires of my heart. The God I serve will do that for you and me. *"…that He may give you the desires of your heart,"* (Psalm 37:4). This is the word of God, and it is in the Bible! It is not just me telling you.

Life must continue, and I continue seeking more of Him. Going to church, I heard that my pastor has not been feeling well. It is something going on with his heart, the doctors say, but I know that God has the last word. I was not feeling well, either. I felt nauseous, with a headache, and very dizzy. My pastor preached awesomely, even though he was sick. He was told by a doctor not to over do it, and he stood up and really let the devil have it! I felt that the preaching was also to me, because I had been attacked ever since I was a little girl with so many illnesses. Even that same night I was sick. I could hardly stand up, and that was what he preached about - our health, and our spiritual battle.

I needed to get to the altar to be prayed for, but it seemed impossible. There were so many people, and there was no way to get around them. Everyone needed God so desperately, as much as I also needed Him. I could not get there, so I stood in the back row, and said, "Lord! I need you right now. I can't get to the front, but I'm back here."

God knows! The pastor started saying these words, as he was full of the Holy Spirit at that moment, "Because you have asked me, my daughter, I will give it to you. I give you the gift of miracles!" He said some other things, but I just kept my eyes shut and listened. I remember saying, "Oh, wow! How awesome!" When the service was over, two women came to me and said, "That was you that God was talking to."

"What did He say? I ask because I only heard a little of it. I was way in the back, but I started feeling all safe and warm, all around me." She said, "Yes it was you." As I went down the stairs of the church, another woman stopped me and said the same thing again. I said, "Wow! I needed to hear this confirmation!"

I thought, "Wow! How beautiful God is!" As I was getting ready to go home, the pastor had one of the ushers call for me, and brought me into his office. To my surprise the pastor, still under that powerful anointing, said these words to me, "You were the one that God was talking to! You were the one I saw. He gave you a wonderful gift today. He gave you the gift of miracles! He also said you do not have to do anything! The gift of miracles manifests itself when the Lord is going to give out miracles, so do not worry! He said I will show you when and how that gift will manifest itself."

I praise God so much because he loves me so and He takes care of all my needs, "*And my God will supply all your needs according to His riches in glory by Christ Jesus*" (Philippians 4:19).

Life is difficult, but we all try to live one day at a time. We cannot worry about the next day. "*Therefore do not worry about tomorrow*" (Matthew 6:34). In

June that year the Lord spoke to me again. He called me, "a cup of honor for my faithfulness". He also spoke to me about my oldest son, and how He was changing him. He told my husband that he was going to travel. Praise God, because we have been praying for a mission trip that we want to go to in Venezuela! We will see if it is the Lord's will that we go. The Lord is so good! He has moved me to another spiritual level. I know it, and I feel it, and see it in my life.

Now after all that has happened in my spiritual growth, I have been given the honor of serving as a minister of the altar. What this entailed is when the pastor, or any preacher, finishes preaching, he makes an altar call. We, as ministers, help the pastor in all movements of the altar, and the spiritual moves of God through the pastor. I think that is a great privilege, to be able to minister to others, just like the Lord had been telling me, and preparing me for so long. Now the Lord said to me, "I have opened windows to the spirit world. I am showing you little by little the spiritual world. I will show you things; not for you to tell people, but so that you pray for them." The Lord said to me, "Ask, and I will give you." *"Ask and it will be given to you"* (Matthew 7:7).

6 CHAPTER SIX

The Lord has been doing so much in my life that if I was to write it all down, I would never finish writing! One thing that I want to say, and that I must say is, through all these blessings and miracles, don't think for a minute that it has been easy or all peaceful. No! Not for a minute. The enemy has tried so hard to knock me down. Through all of this, I have had a lot of pain and tribulation, but I have the peace of God to help deal with anything that may come my way. *"Peace I leave with you, My peace I give to you; not as the world gives do I give to you. Let not your heart be troubled, neither let it be afraid"* (John 14:27). That is why it is so important that your faith stays strong, and that you never weaken. It is only that faith that will keep you going forward, strong! And never, ever, forget the blood that Jesus shed for you and me - for there is power in the blood.

Remember the kingdom of God is not for the weak, but for the strong. Be strong through Jesus Christ. When you feel that the enemy comes at you with all his might remember *"The Lord is your keeper; The Lord is your shade at your right hand. The sun shall not strike you by day or the moon by night. The Lord shall preserve you from all evil; He shall preserve your soul. The Lord shall preserve your going out and your coming in from this time forth, and even forevermore"* (Psalm 121:5-

8). This has helped me so much. The Lord has told me so clearly that He is the powerful one, not the enemy. Remember, he that is with you is more powerful than the one that is coming against you.

As I keep reminiscing about all my experiences with God, I remember one occasion at tax time. You know I have learned that in the spirit world there is no such thing as coincidence. God is always in control. There is a purpose and a plan for everything in your life. It's like this book that I am writing: I have no idea who will read it, or where it may wind up. But one thing I do know is that God is in control of everything, and this book will help edify someone, in one way or another! Of that I am truly sure! I am sure of the wonders and glories of God.

Well, it was time to do my taxes, and like you, we got all our paperwork together and took it to our accountant…a normal routine, again, or so I thought. My accountant is a daughter of an awesome woman of God, one who the Lord uses in prophecy, among other things. As I was waiting there for my accountant, so was her mother. We stared back and forth at each other, and finally she came over to speak with me.

We started talking about God, and how great He is. She came over to me, and said, "Sister, I have to pray for you. I don't know what it is, but we will let the spirit guide us." She read the Bible and started praying. She said these words, "I have to anoint you with oil from head to toe, for a purpose." So she anointed me, and prayed for both my husband and me.

The Lord spoke to me that day. *"Samuel took a flask of oil"* (1 Samuel 10:1). "He said I have anointed you for a purpose. I have chosen you! I will show you new things, and I give you a fresh anointing - a new anointing. Where your feet step there will be blessings!" I felt such a nice, warm feeling. I don't know how many of you have experienced something like this, but it felt as when David was anointed by Samuel. It was as if I was being separated for something so special. He said, "Where I send you, you will speak my word."

It is so great to know that Jesus is alive, that he is interceding for us in a powerful way and he is interested in your life. You must understand one thing: we are in a battle that will only end when we go home to dwell with the Lord. The Bible says, *"These things I have spoken to you, that in Me you may have peace. In the world you will have tribulation; but be of good cheer, I have overcome the world."* Jesus died for us, and he arose again on the third day. So you have to believe, my brothers and sisters that those who wait and trust in the Lord are like the eagle - they will soar. I know that it is not easy. Nobody said it was going to be easy; but one thing I do know from experience is that, *"I can do all thing through Jesus Christ"* (Philippians 4:13).

When the Lord calls you, He will confirm that calling on your life maybe one or two times; however, I know myself! I fear my God, and respect him so much that I will never move unless He tells me to go, and I know, and I'm sure that it is Him.

The Lord dealt with me again. I felt that I was in a training camp where I was being taught one on one, what a special feeling. I tell you, you who are reading this book look for a church where the power of God moves freely and powerfully! This will help you grow and train for when you are ready. Only then will your calling come to pass. I remember when my pastor told me, "The Lord is going to use you powerfully in a healing ministry." I thought, wow!

I was very proud of myself! Here is the Lord dealing with me, and calling me out. I said, "I will do, God, what you asked of me." So after four years of Bible theology, I finally graduated. Praise God for that honor. I will never forget the day of my graduation - it was May twenty fourth, and the Lord spoke to me. He said, "I will bring you people. I have given you gifts. In my name, and only my name, they will be healed. Use what I have given you." "...*and I will heal them*" (Matthew 13:15). "Mighty things you will do in my name."

We all go through many things, troubling things, whether it is the death of a loved one, or you grew up without a father or mother. You know the Spirit of the Lord is with you and He will heal you and cause the pain to pass. He will comfort you, just like it says in His word. *"For the word of God is living and active..."* (Hebrews 4:12). Also, "Oh, taste and see that the LORD is good; Blessed is the man who trusts in Him!" (Psalm 34:8). We just have to get into the word of God. In the Bible, in the Scriptures, there you find power. Never ever forget that. Remember to worship the Lord. I believe very strongly in this. Worship is a very important part of your Christian life. You must grow and be strong in the Lord.

The Lord is so faithful to you that He will always let you know when you are in trouble, and also when you have been faithful. *"God is not a man that He should lie,"* (Numbers 23:19). He warns you if you are not headed on the right path, or if our enemy Satan is trying to come at you with a mighty force. I remember at one point in my life going thru a particular ordeal. But I always said, "Lord help me to remain faithful to you." And so, when you are faithful, the Lord will compensate you in many wonderful ways, ways you would never imagine.

I remember in July the Lord spoke to me at church. The pastor was preaching, and after the preaching was over the Lord spoke to me. Let me just say this to you... my pastor is an awesome man of God. He preaches and teaches with such an anointing that only God can give. I know that

God speaks through him, and also that God blesses him, and uses him mightily. That day the Lord said to me, "Because you have been faithful to me, and waited for me, I will give you a miracle. I know your heart, and I know how loyal you have been." *"If you abide in Me, and My words abide in you, you will ask what you desire, and it shall be done for you"* (John 15:7).

My life really has been about getting to know who I am, and who is the God who dwells inside of me. I know now that he has always been there for me. I believe I understand His purpose. It has not been an easy road, but the secret is to remain faithful. Believe me I understand what it is to slip and fall, and in that fall to get a couple of bruises. I know how hard it is after you slip to get back into praising and worshiping God. The devil is not going to make it easy for you. He will strike with full force to try to keep you out. He will discourage you and he will lie. Remember, *"…for he is a liar and the father of all lies"* (John 8:44). He just wants to destroy you, your family and your ministry.

I remember when my oldest son told me he was moving to New York to live with his father. I was so heart broken, because it was so extremely painful for me. I had just come from being with my parents in Puerto Rico for two weeks. There the enemy pounded me for teaching my mother how to be a prayer warrior. He didn't like that, so I came back sick with pneumonia. To put the icing on the cake, my son told me, "I'm leaving, Mom." Talk about no strength! So what can I do here? He is nineteen years old, and really I didn't want to stop him, because I felt it was time. He needed to find out for himself some things in his life that, as his mother I understood, with the Lords help, of course. As you may remember earlier on in this testimony I mentioned to you how much I cried out to God for my older son.

I knew God had opened that door for him at the right time. Still I was sad. I went to church and tried to worship, but couldn't. All I wanted to do was cry. I kept asking the Holy Spirit to intercede for me, to help me get over this period in my life. *"He always lives to intercede for them"* (Hebrew 7:25). I said, "Intercede for me, Holy Spirit." Finally, after many tears shed at the altar, the Lord gave me a comforting word. He said, "I give you strength. Stand up." Then He said, *"For we do not wrestle against flesh and blood, but against principalities, against powers, against the rulers of the darkness of this age, against spiritual hosts of wickedness in the heavenly places"* (Ephesians 6:12). Do not fight or battle any longer for your son. Trust in me for him." So I finally let my son go.

This is very important that you remember. This determines our attitude towards people whenever we are confronted in any manner. For example, when you are driving to work in the morning, and you are running a little late: you have a hard time in the traffic jam. We are not to yell at the other drivers like, "Get out of my way!" and so on. Trust me I know. I have been there. We are to remember our battle is not with the people out there, but with wickedness and spiritual hosts of this time. So next time this happens, stomp on the devil's head and tell him he is a liar, in Jesus' name. I knew I needed to be strong and not be in a pity party all the time. I felt lifted up when I finally figured out who my battle was with.

My son left, and now he is living in New York. I miss him, but God has given me peace. He planted a flag of peace in the midst of my home, and I know that I feel that flag just flowing with a peace that is overwhelming. So I go on with my everyday life, working and living for God first, and my family second. It is very important that you give time to God and to your family. Although my son was leaving me, I knew that he knew who the Lord his God was. My husband and I taught him to always ask God, for he will never leave him. He is always faithful.

I said we must continue enjoying life and we must celebrate. In January, I was putting away all of the Christmas stuff, and I don't know how it happened, but I somehow hurt my back. I was fine. I was sitting on the floor picking up all those little things that fall off the tree. When I stood up, I felt a small discomfort in my back. As the day went on, my back got worse and worse. The pain was just unbearable. I was in pure agony. A couple from church came to pray for me, they had heard I was sick. But really, it is so nice to have people in church, truly brothers and sisters in Christ that care for your needs. Well this couple is like that. They prayed, and the Lord said to me not to overwhelm myself. He said rest in Him. *"...and I will give you rest"* (Matthew 11:28).

My body was still in so much pain, I was already starting to walk sideways. I did not panic, I just waited, and accepted the pain, and tried to be comfortable. This was going on for days. One night, I believe it was around the 10th of January, I was sitting at my kitchen table with my husband. We were having dinner, and I said to him, very calm, "Sweetheart, when we are done eating, please, can you take me to emergency?" I could not take the pain anymore, it was so intense that I could not even cry. I wanted to pass out, and was afraid, so I said, "Take me when we are done."

My husband just looked at me in shock. He said, "Are you ok?" I said "No." We went to the hospital. I got there, and my entire side was dropped to the right. They took me in right away. I mean the pain was awful. I was given an IV with some medication. I was also given a shot of painkiller to calm me down. After I was prepped and sort of calmed, they sent me for a test to see if it was kidney stones. As I waited there, while I was being poked and stabbed in the hospital with all kind of needles, I was meditating in the Lord. I kept saying my favorite Psalm. It was in my mind over and over, Psalm 23, "The Lord is my Shepheard, I shall not want."

After all that agony, I said, "Lord, let it be your perfect will in my life. The enemy has always attacked me in my health in a powerful and furious way. But You, oh Lord, are my source of strength, my will, please don't leave me." Honestly, I was scared. When I was a little girl I was paralyzed for a while. I did not want that to come back. My mother told me I had kidney failure, and I did not want that pain, ever again.

Here it was, three thirty in the morning, and I was still in a hospital bed, in pain. I knew that the enemy was trying to put fear in me, and at some point, it was working. But God will never leave you, or forsake you. The test result was in, and there was nothing wrong with me according to the doctor, but I was still in pain. The medication they gave me finally started kicking in.

My husband started talking to the doctor, and here I was, listening to the two of them. The doctor said, "Your wife had surgery on her back a long time ago, and maybe she is just having some kind of reaction to that, like arthritis." My husband very calmly said, "Ok". The doctor said, "Just take her to a back specialist to check her for arthritis."

I looked at them, and I said, "Wait! I have never had back surgery!" The doctor said, "Yes, and you have the scar to prove it." My husband had mentioned to me a long time ago about a scar that I had in the center of my spine, but it just went over my head. As I kept listening to them speak, I just said, "How?" I didn't understand what was being said between the two of them. The doctor said, "The surgery is beautiful," and showed my husband the X-rays.

I came home, still in pain, but more puzzled. I told my husband I have to call my mother. Remember, my mother said I suffered a lot when I was little, and a lot of the things she blocked out of her mind, or else she just does not want to talk about them. But I needed to know! Here I am in pain, all to one side, couldn't straighten up, and I needed to know.

I called my mother and explained to her what was going on, and what the doctor had said about my scar on my back. She started telling me that when I was around thirteen or fourteen years old, I fell on the floor with a terrible pain in my back. The doctors had told my mother that I had a bad back, and that many things could happen to me; for me to take things slow. I remember going to my doctor and the doctor telling my mom, "Your daughter can't even mop the floor." By now I was totally in shock, as you can imagine.

My mother said, "Norma, you always had a bad back. When you were little you could not walk, so they took liquid out of your spine to put in your knees. That didn't help you." I thought, "That's the scar." My husband said, "No, the scar is about an inch long."

My mother kept telling me, "One night, we were all having dinner. It was around seven at night when you fell to the floor. You were in so much pain. You couldn't stop crying because of the pain," she said. My mother and my father tried to get me up on my feet, but they couldn't. My mother told my father, "Let's pray for her that God will heal her once and for all of this back pain." So they prayed, and rebuked the enemy over my life. After much prayer, I stopped crying, and I stood up. My mother said to me that was the last time that my back bothered me. This was great because I knew then the miracle that God had performed on me. Another miracle! God, He is so awesome.

As time went on, I understood more and more the battles that we as Christians encounter. Here I was, and I felt well from my back; however, I was still in some pain. I said to myself, "Know what?" That Monday, my church was invited to join and fellowship in a special service in another church. My pastor told me, "Today you are not going to work at the altar. So sit down, and receive, and enjoy the service." I was so hurt, because I wanted to be at the altar so badly! I knew the anointing. I felt His presence, and I desired so much to be there, closer to Him.

I wanted to be prayed for that night. I was standing up, but so crooked that the pain was horrible. This time it was in my stomach, so I went up to the altar and asked my pastor's wife for prayer. She went to get oil to pray for me, and as my eyes were closed, all of a sudden I fell backwards. It was as if I was in slow motion, falling down to the floor. It felt like while I was praying, I fell back, and it was as if I was in a bed of clouds! That's how soft it was. While I was on the floor, I was laughing with such joy, as if someone was making me giggle! My husband told me that it looked like a lot of hands were tickling me from the movements that I was making. My pastor, who was really far from me, ran down towards where I was. As he came over, he started praying for me.

There was such silence in that place. I heard the Lord my God speak to me. He said, "The enemy has attacked you, through your finances, but mostly your health, and you know it. He is so afraid of you my servant! He knows the potential that I have put in you. He knows the powerful anointing that I have placed in you, and given you. I say to you that where you go, there will be miracles and healing. The enemy knows this, and he looks at you from afar, because he cannot come near to you. He knows who you are, that is why you are attacked!"

When I heard this, I remembered the story of the two disciples that went to rebuke demons in the Bible. The demons spoke to them, and said, *"Jesus we know. Paul we know. But you we don't know,"* (Acts 19:13-16). Can you imagine the authority that God places on you for battle? God said, "You have a powerful anointing that I have given you. Use it!" There was victory that night! I stood up, and was completely healed. I was straight, no pain, just feeling great. Again, God gets the glory of all my healing miracles.

I remember calling out to my husband, who was watching from a little distance, "Sweetheart! Look, I am healed!" He was just as happy as I was. How many of you know that we serve a mighty and powerful God. He knows all of our needs. I have tried all my life to understand why certain things happen to me, and to all of us. It stuns me to see the way that God has an answer for every little thing that happens in our lives in His Word! It just amazes me to see that for every bad thing that the enemy tries to send our way, there is a good thing that God does that comes out of any situation.

Ours is not to try-and-worry-so-much to understand; but rather, just to do as He says and obey Him. I have learned that we have a choice to make: we can choose the easy way with God, and all of His benefits; or choose the hard way, with the enemy, and be alone in this world, with the enemy constantly lying, cheating, and just doing horrible things to you. I would do the smart thing and choose God, and all of His wonderful promises and rewards, like the Bible clearly states.

It is so wonderful to feel the Lord's presence and to be under His anointing. There is nothing like it. I have learned how to enjoy all that God has given me, and all of His benefits. I know that it has been hard, because the enemy does not leave you alone for one minute, and you are in constant battle; however with God all things are possible. *"But He said, 'The things which are impossible with men are possible with God'"* (Luke 18:27). So my advice to you is don't give up - not for a minute. I am right there with you. I also am just starting out. I will tell you what: the first thing that the Lord put in my heart was to write down every experience that I had with Him, so I did just that. That is why I am now telling you, and sharing with you, most of my experiences.

Never give up on God! Hang in there, and remember that there is a Spirit inside of you that desires to just worship. All he is asking is for you to let Him. Let Him do what God has ordained Him to do in you, and for you. Any and every chance that you have, pray in the spirit, so that this way you can be lifted up. Trust in God with all your might, and He will never disappoint you.

God still keeps on working in our lives - in yours and in mine. He never stops, and will never stop. Once I was invited to a women's retreat here locally. I really debated whether I should go or not. Finally I said ok. It was Friday afternoon when we had the first conference. I told only three women from my church. While I was in church, I saw these two women I know. I heard the Lord tell me in my heart, "Do not be selfish! Go and tell them about this retreat." I was afraid to tell anyone in church, because I thought I would get in trouble. It's not easy trying to bring the body of Christ together in unity, (see Ephesians 4:13).

Well, how many of you know that God is in control? To my surprise the two ladies said, "Yes", that they would go. They had actually been praying to have some time away with God. We decided we would meet there. It was awesome!

The first service was with a powerful lady. She spoke about **Stirring up the Gifts**. It was a powerful teaching. She read many Bible verses, but the one that she focused on was 2 Timothy 1:6, *"Wherefore I put thee in remembrance that thou stir up the gift of God, which is in thee by the putting on of hands."* The Lord is so great because He knows exactly what you need. He knows the desires of your heart, and all He wants to do is make you happy.

We all went home that night feeling mighty grateful to God and full of His love. Saturday morning came along, and at 9:00 A.M. we were in the first conference. I had prayed the night before, and asked God to guide me as to which conference to go to. I let my spirit-man guide me, and He was right on. The woman spoke on **The Spirit Man**! It was a topic about letting your spirit man out. In other words, God fills you up; He gives you gifts and talents, and then when you are ready, The Holy Spirit starts trying to do what He must do. Except that we are so proud, sometimes, that we just don't let Him out.

We feel we can do everything on our own. God was trying to say to us, "It is time you let me do what I want to do, and have been trying to do, in your life. Allow me to do it!" The Lord fills you up; then your spirit is ready to go out, and either preach or speak or do whatever your calling is upon your life. *"Neglect not the gift that is in thee, which was given thee by prophesy, with the laying on of the hands of the presbytery"* (1 Timothy 4:14).

After the speaker was done, there was an awesome anointing in the place. We all fell into that wonderful anointing. Let me tell you about the anointing: it is like wonderful warmth that comes over you, and you feel so safe, and so strong at the same time. The Lord started ministering to us in such a powerful way. I remember sitting down and crying so much! This lady came around me, and lifted up my arms, like when Moses' hands became weary. He could not keep his hands up, so *"Aaron and Ur lifted them up for him"* (Exodus 17:12). The Lord said to me, "Stand up! You cannot do what I have asked of you sitting down." Those were powerful words. Praise the living God! I had been contemplating sitting down at my church; not serving, not doing anything but listening to preaching, and just being still. I understood that was not what God wanted for me to do.

Saturday evening came, and we went to the next conference. This conference was with the same woman of God that gave us the first conference. The title of this conference was **The Midnight Call**. It was also powerful, with such great anointing. She read the parable of the wise and foolish virgins from Matthew 25. She spoke on how we have to be ready for that midnight call, and be ready for the yell of, "The Bride Groom is coming!" It was so wonderful the way that she taught it. I just love to hear a woman of God speak with such authority. By the time she finished preaching and ministering we were all on the floor.

God just spoke to me so strongly again about the calling that is on my life. I always asked God about my calling. I used to ask, just as I am sure many of you ask yourself this question - "What is my calling?" Although God tells you, we still want to hear Him say what our calling is. I admire those people that the Lord gives them a calling, and they just "know that they know" that it's Gods calling upon their life.

By this time, you know that I am so excited in the Lord, for we have had an unbelievable weekend. At nighttime, I asked my husband to join me at the last general session. We were told that the husbands could come if they wanted. So I called him, and he said sure. That evening, it was at seven o'clock that the service started. It was very good. The worship and the word that was ministered was about dreams, and the gift of interpreting dreams. She read from many books of the Bible; from the New Testament to the Old Testament, from Joseph to Paul. It was so powerful.

She started asking us if we had that gift of interpreting dreams. Then she said, "Why not?" Why can't you and I have that gift? Dreams are a way that God uses to communicate with his people, and as we all know, God is the same always. We serve the same God. If he did it back then, he is still doing it today. It's just that there are so many psychic phone lines doing now what God uses for his purposes. Satan has taken control of it, and he is using it against the people, and the body of Christ. This has been taken for granted that it is ok to interpret dreams. For example, *"But God came to Abemilech in a dream"* (Genesis 20:3). This is one of many scriptures in the Bible where God showed himself to many people thru dreams.

There are many ways to interpret dreams. I was so overwhelmed, because I was really never taught about this. I knew that God speaks to you in a dream, but that it was ok to interpret dreams was something else! I understand now that The Lord my God will use any means possible to get his message across to his people. He was doing it back in the Old Testament, and He is still doing it now.

We could mention so many scriptures, from Genesis to the last book of the Bible Revelation, and show you that it has so many dreams. But let that be a homework assignment that you do on your own time, praise God. I learned so much when I decided to let God do in my life what he wanted, what He had planned all along, when I stopped fighting him on every issue. I tell you - make a decision and stick to it! Say to yourself, and really mean it, "I will stop fighting with God's every word, and every way, and I will let God do as He wants in my life."

When the preacher finished preaching her message on dreams, she said,

"The Lord wants to minister to people here that don't know him yet, or that somehow feel that they need to get closer to him." She also said, "If you do not stand up, because you know who you are, God will call you out." As soon as she said those words she called this man out who was sitting in the back with his wife. The Lord spoke to him of a calling on his life to be a pastor. It was great, because earlier, in the morning that same day, someone else called him out and said the same thing to him. So there was a confirmation from the Lord upon this man's life. She finished with this gentleman, then she called out my husband and me.

The Lord had a word for us. She said to my husband, "Did you know that you were a teacher?" My husband shook his head in a "no" fashion. She continued, saying, "There is an awesome calling upon your life. You will go, and speak to nations; you will minister and preach to many." My husband was in a state of numbness. He was just receiving the word. This had been told to my husband before. When the service was over, the preacher that had ministered to me came over to speak to me and say hello. She was so sweet. She came over to my husband and said, "Let me shake the hand of such a powerful man of God!" My husband just looked at her. She went on, saying to us, "When the two of you walked into the service, there was this glow that came in with you." It was just wonderful, because that was how we felt, like we were wrapped in warmth

Another thing that happened was that the lady that had preached about the dreams, and had also called my husband and I up to the altar, said to us, "There is something about the two of you. You are going to have a powerful ministry. When the two of you came into the room there was a glow that walked in with you."

She repeated the same words that the other preacher had said!

Coincidence? I don't think so! I think God was taking a stand, and saying this is it in our lives. Look how our Father God works: when I was growing up, in my youth years, I always had this strange dream. This was a dream that every now and then I would dream it. I decided to tell my dream to the lady who had that gift of interpreting dreams. I told my husband this was the perfect time to find out what this dream that constantly came upon me meant. My husband knew the dream, because I had told him about it so many times. I feel that when something is this powerful in your life, you should tell someone. This way, when it comes to pass, you and the person will know that this was God.

So, I was brave and started telling her the dream. It went as follows: I always dreamed that I was surrounded by water, and there were all kinds of fish, all sizes, and all shapes in it. This was in a large body of water. I am not sure whether it was in a pond, or an ocean, but there they are, always. This to me was so frightening! As I walked into this large, massive body of water, or as I looked into a tank, or when I see them all around me. It became a nightmare to me. It was so bad that I could not get into the ocean at the beach, or go to any aquarium.

To my surprise my younger son came to me one day and said, "Mom, I have been dreaming about fish all around me." Now he is starting to be afraid of the ocean, and the fish. I told this to this lady, I told her of my constant fear. She asked me a question. She asked, "Why are you afraid of fish?" She said, "The Lord said in Mark 1:17, *'I will make you fishers of men.'* The reason why this bothers you so is because the Lord has been calling you to do this. The fish in the Bible represent men, and you have been called for this. You have to obey your calling, and say "Yes" to God. The reason why now your son is having the dreams is because he is calling your whole family."

I was, as you know, just totally grateful. I felt so much taken out of me, like so much weight lifted from me, as I stood there and understood what for so many years I could not understand before.

I know that most of us have been going through a lot of turmoil. It has not been an easy time, but you know it is all worth it. *"The Lord is our strength,"* (Psalm 27:1). In all the things that we see and do and go through, God is there to make sure that we come through with flying colors.

All my days, my life has been one thing after the other. Don't think for one minute that it has been easy. You know I heard a preacher once say, "I do not like people that preach to you, and tell you, 'Repent and all your troubles will be simple or things will be so much better.' She went on, saying, "You have to say the truth, and not lie to people: Things will get worse!"

But with God, things are so much easier, because He gives you *peace in abundance.* It is in the Bible, Psalm 37:11. You just have to learn how to apply the Word of God to your life. There is an answer to any question that you may have. Trust in God, and you will see. He will do for you what He promised you He would do, just like me. Sunday we had a terrific service; it was a service for miracles. I love those services because the Holy Spirit manifests in such an awesome way. I went for prayer, and I felt so good! Not like I got a miracle, but like I received more anointing. I started letting the Lord use me, and just like He has promised, He used me in a powerful way.

I prayed for so many women, and they were all on the floor, one by one, full of the anointing of God. I was so amazed to see something that God had said to me come to pass. He said, "I will use you to do powerful things." To actually stand there, turn around and see all these people on the floor, full of anointing, was such a wonderful thing. I obeyed God, and did what He told me to do, and His spirit moved in a powerful way. The glory and the honor is to God! He is the one that I love, and who deserves everything. I recognize that without God, I am nothing.

Everything that happens in your life, as well as in my life, is solely for a purpose. Don't ever think, or doubt in your mind, that the things that happen are because you are under a black cloud, or that bad luck is just following you around. In the realm of God there is no bad luck or black cloud. Things happen because there is a purpose for your life and everything that happens in your life, the Lord our God has allowed it. This is so that we become stronger individuals, and so that we can help others that are perhaps going through the same situation that you and I were going through, or already went through. Always, above everything, remember, *"What then shall we say to these things? If God is for us, who can be against us?"* (Romans 8:31).

I just experienced something so awesome, that you will understand how God works in mysterious ways. These are ways that we don't even know about yet, but we can feel and know that it is God. We have been invited to go to a pastor's and leaders' conference, my husband and I. There are many reasons why, in the world's point of view, we cannot go. Number one is my husband is in the kind of a job where you take your vacations once or twice a year and that is it. He has already taken his vacation for this year. In order for my husband to get time off from work would only be by a miracle. Well, he asked his Lieutenant, and he said, "Yes, no problem." That in itself is miracle number one. The Lord opened doors for my husband to go on this trip. Number two, we needed money for the airline tickets. At that moment, I was unemployed and we were working on a budget. My husband called the airline, and they gave him a price for a round trip ticket for both of us. My husband told me, "Call the airlines and get the tickets." When I called, the price of the tickets was half of what they had originally given us! That was miracle number two.

Number three: I called the hotel which we were going to stay in. They told me it was booked, and that they had no more availability. I spoke to someone and started mentioning God, and guess what? They were touched and gave us a room! When I came home, I had applied for a job that would become a great blessing. This was miracle number four. This was the way that the Lord covered all of our financial needs when we came back from this trip.

The reason I am telling you this testimony is because I know that there are some of you out there that need to hear how God makes all things possible, if you only have faith, and believe in Him. *"Ask, and it will be given to you; seek, and you will find; knock, and it will be opened to you"* (Mathew 7:7). God's word is truth! He does not tell a lie. I am living proof of all of His wonderful blessings. I know that sometimes it is extremely hard for you to believe, and the devil is not going to make it easy for you. But you need only to trust in God, and in His word.

There is an answer for you in His word, if you only give Him time, and believe in Him, believe in Jesus Christ His son - and all things are possible! I was in church this one morning, and there was such an awesome anointing in the house of God. I just wanted to throw myself on my knees and praise Him. The Lord gave me a word. He said to me, "For I have anointed you, and pre-ordained you for such a time as this." I was so overwhelmed I could hardly stand. I quickly wrote it down, and showed it to my husband when I heard another word that said, "The Preacher today will confirm this word!" You just cannot imagine how I felt.

We stood up and the preacher said to us, "Look in your Bible in 1 Samuel 16. This talks about David's anointing with oil, and it speaks about Bethel, the place of calling."

You know that God makes the impossible possible. How was I ever going to think that this preacher was going to confirm a word from God that I needed? But you see, the Lord God that I know is famous for doing things like this. We are always thinking to ourselves, "It is impossible for God to do something like that," and yet that is the way He works! Praise Him! He is all glory and power, forever, amen.

7 CHAPTER SEVEN

I hope that this can help you to understand yourself a lot better. I know that we're put on this earth with a purpose and a reason. There is a purpose for you, and only God knows that purpose. It is up to you if you want to fulfill your destiny in the Lord, and take back all that the enemy has taken from you. Remember that God is in control of everything, and there hasn't been a battle that He has not won.

Our God is an awesome God, and He has angels at His command that will fight for you. You know, that for each one of us, if you could only visualize the spiritual world, you would see the awesome army of God fighting constantly for you, protecting you against all the traps and turmoils of the enemy. You see you are very special, and important to God, and once you surrender everything to Him He will fight for you. Even if you don't surrender to Him, He still watches over you, and patiently waits for the day that you say, "Yes, Father - I surrender all."

I have learned to praise my God in the good times and in the bad times. God wants you to sacrifice worship to Him. He loves for you to worship Him. He loves your praises. I have had experiences where I just start singing in my house, and just praising Him, and the warmth that I feel is just so overwhelming. The desire to be in His presence becomes an obsession, only because I know that in Psalm 16:11 it says, *"You will show me the path of life; In Your presence is fullness of joy; At Your right hand are pleasures forevermore."* So I live to serve Him, and just to do what He wants me to do, to please Him in any way. You have to understand, He has given me eternal life, and that to me is worth a lot. So I give Him thanks, and I rejoice in Him who created the heavens and the earth (see Genesis 1).

My advice to you is read the Bible, pray to the Lord your God, and praise Him. But remember, the enemy is going to try everything possible to stop you. You see, the enemy knows the potential that there is in you. He knows that there is an awesome power, and anointing, that God has placed on you. Remember that the devil was the angel of light. God created him, and he was beautiful. Read the book of Genesis. The Lord's glory was over him until he tried to take over God's position - he wanted to be God. The devil hates you so much, because of 1 Corinthians 3:16, *"Do you not know that you are the temple of God and that the Spirit of God dwells in you?"* You are a powerful person; you have God's anointing. The things that were his, God gave them to you. Now you know, the devil is going to try to take all that away from you, to shame you until you have nothing. Do not worry - that's why we are children of the light, and not of darkness.

So I tell you guard yourself. *"Be sober; be vigilant; because your adversary the devil walks about like a roaring lion, seeking whom he may devour"* (1 Peter 5:8). The Bible says this! But fear not, for the Bible also says, *"What then shall we say to these things? If God is for us, who can be against us?"* (Romans 8:31). Believe, brothers and sisters! Believe in God and you will see His glory, and the difference in your life. Do not be afraid, and trust in God with all your might. Surrender everything to Him.

I feel like praying right now for some of you who feel touched, at this point, by God. I feel the Spirit of God guiding me to pray for someone who has not totally surrendered everything to God yet, for one reason or another. Only you know why. You must believe, and, *"If we confess our sins, He is faithful and just to forgive us our sins and to cleanse us form all unrighteousness"* (1 John 1:9).

Say this prayer with me:

> Father in the name of Jesus, I come before you. You know my heart, the deepest part of my soul. Lord cleanse me with your blood, the blood that your son Jesus shed for me on the cross. Lord I ask that you renew me. Renew my spirit. Lord I am an open vessel for your glory! Come into my heart, and fill me up with your Holy Spirit. Lord I ask that you plant a seal on my forehead, because Lord, I am your property. I do not want to serve this world; this world has nothing for me. I only desire you, Father. Here I am! Forgive me! In the name of the Father, the Son and the Holy Ghost, amen.

Just give God praise. I don't know about you, but I always feel good praying! Thank you Jesus. *"Grace, mercy, and peace will be with you from God the Father and from the Lord Jesus Christ, the Son of the Father, in truth and love"* (2 John 1:3). Amen. Remember, we can't all do the same things. I know that you have a talent that God gave you for the purpose of using you. Pray, read the Word of God, and He will bring you out like a beautiful flower ready to be picked. *"…and he gave some, apostles; and some, prophets; and some, evangelists; and some, pastors and teachers"* (Ephesians 4:11). This means we are a body with one purpose, but many callings. The Lord wants to use you and me in many wonderful and powerful ways. But you must remain faithful to Him always.

One Sunday, I went to church as usual. I was kind of sad, yet, at the same time, sort of on the alert, waiting and waiting. How many of you know that when God is getting ready to do something in your life, things just don't happen by chance, or by coincidence. I was in the morning service at the church where I went, and I was feeling such a powerful anointing during the worship service. I was praising God, and all of a sudden I felt the Lord speak to me, and put a word in my heart. I said, "God, is this you?"

The night service was just as great, and I was so full of the presence of the Lord. It was as if I was in a totally different world, if you can relate to that. The time that you spend with God in His presence it's like being at a party.

I had a great experience that following Tuesday. My husband and I went to listen to a lady preacher from Tampa, Florida. It was so good. She preached with so much love towards God, and the Word of God. I was sitting with my husband, and after she preached again on David and his anointing, I figured out that God definitely was trying to tell us something. I was right! The Lord spoke to us about our calling, and all of the things that the enemy had taken away. He spoke about how He was going to return them to us at seven fold, not two, and He said many other wonderful things. I was very happy, because we always should look for confirmation from God. I will not worry. I know my life has a purpose, and only God knows that.

We are just to wait patiently for Him, and He will do what He has to do. He will open or close whatever door He has to open or close. This, of course, is all in the spiritual world, as well as the secular world. I trust Him with all my strength, and have faith that He knows what is good for me, for He is my source of strength. After all, He is my Heavenly Father. Like the book of Isaiah says, *"He who waits upon the Lord will soar like an eagle"* (Isaiah

40:31). I believe it because it is the word of God. I tell you remain faithful to the Lord and He will come through for you. Just trust in Him.

I just came back from a Pastors' and Leaders' conference. This was the very first one that I have ever gone to. I always obey God. He said to me one day, "When they invite you, do not say no, for it is I who send you." I believed Him, so when my Pastor asked my husband, he said, "Yes". At first, I went through all that emotion of, "How! God how?" Then I remembered His words, and just let Him do it. Glory be to God, we went! We had a great time. We learned a lot about leaders, and loyalty, and also the way to follow and submit yourself to God first. It was really good, and interesting. I always look for ways in which God tries to show me something. I think that is a very good habit to get into.

If anything, always look for a blessing in your day. Remember, the Bible does say about His blessings, *"They are new every morning; Great is Your faithfulness,"* (Lamentations 3:23). Just the way the morning dew is fresh every morning, so are God's promises for you and me. We must learn from all these experiences so that we can teach others who are just starting out on this path.

I often wonder if I am the only one that goes through so many things? But as you and I know, we are not alone. I thank God for all His blessings. I have been going to see a Preacher who has devoted her life to God, and travels from such a far place to come to us once a month to give us the word of God.

She is truly a woman who loves the Lord. Her name is Carol Elaine; she has truly been an inspiration to my family and me. I want you to know that when you are at your loneliest times, God always finds and sends someone to you so that you will not be alone. That is what Carol was for me. She has been a blessing. This New Year is a year of blessings. This is my year, said God. He told me this on Sunday as my pastor was preaching.

The pastor said, "I will anoint everyone here, because the Lord said to do so." As he was praying for me he said, "The Lord said, 'This is your year'." I was so excited to hear those words. I had been waiting for those words for such a long while. Then, praise God, here it was, Friday night of the same week, and I was invited to my pastor's wife's home for an appreciation dinner. As we prayed, again, the Lord spoke to me and said to me, "This is your year." He actually confirmed what He had said that Sunday. I was in a cloud of total, anointing ecstasy. God has been so good to me, so far, and he has never failed me. I am a strong believer in all of His promises.

A lot has happened in the last couple of months, I am no longer an altar minister. I have decided to sit down for a while and receive from the Lord. It has not been an easy time for me. I have been going through a lot of things, but the God that I know has not forsaken me at all. He has been my strength at this point in my life. He has been talking to me, and still it has been a prophetic word that he has confirmed to me.

I have been praying that God just holds on to me and not let me go. We have to have faith, and hold on to all the words and promises that are in the Bible. The Lord has given me so many prophetic words, on so many different issues in my life, that I have to believe and have faith that he will pull me through.

I went to a women's conference. I had to mention to you prior, and I also said, that I was looking for a word of God as to what He would have me do. To tell you the truth, and I'm sure you are well aware of this also, it is not easy waiting, or trying to figure out, "What is it Lord?" I had been fighting with myself, and I had not let God deal with my own, personal heart. This had been coming for quite a while. This was a very hard time, because it was just not easy to let all of my personal feelings go, and to let God do what He had to do in me.

I was taught at this time in my life that I cannot move unless He tells me to move. *"Be still, and know that I am God; I will be exalted among the nations, I will be exalted in the earth! "* (Psalm 46:10). This is what He wants of all of us - to wait in Him! He has our lives all planned out for us. We just have to make sure that we do what He tells us, and also be very sensitive to His voice. He said in His word, *"Ask, and it will be given to you; seek, and you will find; knock, and it will be opened to you"* (Matthew 7:7). Those are very important principals to live by. If anything, remember those three things.

Many things happened within the last year since I decided to sit down, and no longer work in the church. It had been very hard for me to just do nothing. I don't know about you, but I have such a desire in my heart to serve the Lord. I had been trying so hard to do the right thing.

The reason why I sat down was because there was jealousy in the midst of my church. I was being led by the spirit to work, and to speak, and my peers as well as my pastor, the one who gave me so many words from God, did not want me any more in the altar. My husband made a decision, and I agreed with him - it was time to go, to move, to leave to another church. I was hurting inside. Some of you might understand the way that I felt, while others might not. All my life I have known the Lord, and all my life up to that point I had never left a church because of problems with anyone. To me this was so unbelievable, and hard to accept.

I prayed, and I fasted, and finally, I just left. We stayed home, and did not go to any other church. I thought, "What am I going to go to another church for?" But, deep in my heart, there was a passion for God and the Holy Spirit! I missed it. I wanted that fire that burned in my bones to be there again. We decided, my husband and I, to go to another church. We went, and it was not right. I felt kind of out of place, as if I was homeless.

These were trying times. I knew it. I thank God that in everything that we go through, He is right there, teaching us a lesson. Because, you must understand one thing - God is always teaching us. In everything that we do there is a lesson to be learned. In all this trying time, I was home, not going to any church. My son, the smallest one, had just turned eighteen. So he decided to leave home.

When he left I was totally heart broken. I thought about everything that had happened to me, and then on top of that, my little son, who to me was still a baby, left - and not on good terms. I know many of you are thinking, "Well, he was old enough." I am here to tell you as a mother, and as mothers we all know when our kids are ready to leave, or not. Trust me - he was not ready to move out.

I prayed, and prayed, asking God to please watch over him. I used to spend hours in the night crying for him, and was so sad all the time. I think it was around six months, and I had not seen him, or heard from him. You've got to understand, in all these trying times God was there with me; He never left me alone for one minute. God knew. He knows how much you can handle.

I was always praying and asking God for a protection for my sons because I did not know what to think, or what to do. I remember it was Mother's

Day, and I just dread that day. I knew my boys were gone and I was all alone with my husband. Well, my husband wanted me to have a good time, so he wanted to take me out to eat. I was crying all that morning. I started getting dressed and the doorbell rang. It was my son!

He actually bought me flowers, came just for a second, and then he left. I looked at those flowers, and I just cried, and cried, and cried. It was so terrible. My boy! I wanted to hug him, talk to him, but there was something so terrible on him that he just could not stay. He was so tied up by the enemy, he could not even look at me in the face. But we all know that the devil cannot look at you in your face. So I understood that my son was at war with the enemy, and so was I.

After that Mother's Day, I did not see him again for a while. Then one day, my husband saw him at a store. My son spoke to his dad, and said, "Can I come home and have my favorite dinner?" I felt like the prodigal son was coming home! And, my dear friends, that is exactly what happened. My son, little by little, came back home. I thank God for all of His wisdom to be able to handle all of this.

I have learned that all of it is a learning process. Everything that goes on in your daily, routine life is an experience, so that you will be able to help someone else in the near future, who at some point will be going through that. A couple of months into my dilemma with my son, a friend of mine started with the same problem with her eighteen year old son. We were able to comfort each other through Christ, who was, and is, our source of strength.

I continue with what God has called me to do. I am the President of Spanish Aglow International East. It has been a battle, but here I am. I was given this honor by God who called me. He told me one day to tend his sheep. I will never forget when I heard that, I cried so much. He said, "Tend to my sheep, for they are so hurt. Tend to them, and I will give you words of comfort for them, for I am the light that shines in the midst of the darkness."

That was so unforgettable! I said, "Yes", and here I am for now until God tells me any different. I am a very passionate woman when it comes to God's things as you have noticed. Becoming the President of Spanish Aglow is an honor, for whatever reason I am here to learn and grow. I was doing what He called me to do; God was using me mightily and teaching me constantly. After much debate, and questions from Aglow, I realize I have to step down. This decision came after much prayer, and asking God again for His guidance.

I remember sitting in the office in my house. I was crying and praying. I could not believe all the things I have gone through. I now know that this is all a learning process that I had to go through. As I continued praying, the Lord spoke to my heart and I heard so clearly, "Entre Amigas," which means 'among friends'. I pondered, and I realized that among friends we could do so much. The Lord put the idea into my head of a powerful ministry. I went online and registered the ministry. I named it Entre Amigas, and I have been doing this since then.

I thank God, because even though I have been attacked by the enemy in all directions, He has been faithful to me. We have had many wonderful speakers, and many wonderful ministries. Through it all, it is always God who gets the honor and the Glory. Through all this, I lost my dad. He passed on, or better yet he moved to heaven. My dad, who I learned to love throughout the years, is now in heaven. It was an honor, as an ordained minister of the Word, to facilitate my dad's funeral, his memorial service and gravesite service. Thank you, God, for honoring me, and allowing me to come full circle with my dad. Love you daddy.

My father's passing took a big toll on me. I almost lost it all. When I said all, I meant all. I was tired, beaten and so hurt. I thought, how could my dad die? I prayed to God not to take him. We fought for a year with his illness. Doctors did not know what was wrong with him. They would tell us all kinds of stories, but never the truth. It was devastating. The enemy telling me so many ugly things. It physically and emotionally drained me. I stop doing ministry, and boy did it cost me. We battled against any name that the doctors would say he had. They came up with some beautiful names, examples, pneumonia, infection, you name it. But in reality we won the battle. My father is now in heaven, enjoying all the wonders of God, and walking with saints.

I paid a hefty price for stopping ministry. I had to cry out to Jesus for forgiveness, and I am so glad that he heard my cry. Much has happened since then. I have met, and continue to meet, wonderful and powerful women of God. But now the ministry has changed. God said, "No longer, my daughter, just women…you need the men also, for they are staying home, while their wives come to be with me." Like I said throughout this book, God is always in control. He is my source of strength. The ministry is now called, "Unity of the Faith", according to Ephesians 4:13. To God is the glory, for He is, and continues to be, my source of strength.

God continues teaching me and molding me in all areas of ministry. We have grown; we teach, preach, and work in all areas of ministry, and continue working for the kingdom. I still travel to the island. I am trying to bring my mom to live with us. Since my dad passed, she is all alone in

Puerto Rico, and that concerns me.

I continue in my work for God, always looking to help, or work, in any and all areas of ministry. I remember this date and it will be very hard to forget. The month of July, oh the pain of that event. I had to have knee surgery, because I somehow injured my left knee. I remember speaking with my mom, and she wanted to come as she normally did, and try to help me with my procedure.

I told my mom, "No worries, I will be fine." I had the surgery July 18, and I was fine, everything came out good, that's what my doctor said. I was coming home from therapy, when I got a phone call from my sister. I hesitated to say it, because in my spirit, I knew it was over. When I answered the phone, there was silence. I said, "Hello," like in a question mark.

My sister was calm. She said, "Norma, Mom has fallen, and she is being taken in a helicopter to a trauma hospital." I could not speak, I was lost. I was hurt, and so confused. We did not know much because she was so far away. We spent the next hours trying to get to my mom. All that time, the Holy Spirit was with me so strong, so great that just like He said in Hebrews 13:5, "*Let your conduct be without covetousness; be content with such things as you have. For He Himself has said, 'I will never leave you nor forsake you.'*"

I finally made it to the hospital. I knew that there was such a battle going on. I thought I was never going to make it. My mother was in an intensive care unit, and the doctors there would not let me see her. She was so badly injured that they did not want anyone to upset her. I was so surprised, I thought to myself, how could she be so badly injured? I battled with all these thoughts in my head for a while, as I desperately tried to get in to see my mother.

The only way they let me in was when I said that I was an ordained minister, and that I had every right to visit her. When I walked in the room, I prayed, I asked God to give me strength. There was a security guard that came in the room with me, for whatever reason they did not trust us, such nonsense I could not believe what I was seeing. But through it all, I knew my battle.

I heard clearly the Holy Spirit. He said to me, "Go and be a minister to your mother. Once you've done what you must do, then you can be her daughter." You must understand the way my mother was, she loved God so much, that I'm sure she wanted to be right by him. So I prayed with her, and gave her communion as best as I could do. When I finished with communion, again I prayed for her, and I said, "Lord, help me! Help me to be with my mom, and help her through this time."

With tears in my eyes, I heard a little small voice that said to me, "Go, be with your mother. You have done what she has asked." I was crying so hard, but I had to compose myself. I saw two hands before me with closed fists, and I heard a voice said, "Choose: Stay or Go". I was in so much pain, I chose for her to go and be with God. I knew the damage in her brain was just too much.

I went over to my mom. I looked at the security guard, and I felt peace. I went over to her ear and I whispered. You have to understand something. You might think people are dead, but the spirit is alive, waiting to hear from God, or a word of release. This is what I was feeling. So I said, "Mom, this is your daughter, Norma. Mom, I love you." My mother was already considered brain dead. The doctors had said she had no brain movement, but we who believe in God know better. So I went close to her, and this was my time with Mom. The moment I told her in her ear, "Go, be with God," her body started shaking, she started trembling, and the security guard said, "This women is alive. She is responding!" I said, "Go with God!" Then there was peace, and it was over.

I knew then that my mother's spirit had parted to be with God. I was numb after that, just waiting around for her body to shut down. The doctors wanted to unplug her because she wasn't on life-support, but I told him, "Could you please do me this one favor?" You know what? They granted me the favor. I said, "Could you not disconnect her, and let her go at her own time?" I said, "Only God can make that choice, not us."

God was a big deal for my mom, and I'm so grateful to him that he took her in peace, that she never knew what happened, or how she moved on. The minute my mother fell, she was in a coma, and she never came out of it. So, I praise God for that. She never knew what happened to her, and she went in peace.

When I was waiting for my mother's body to shut down, a nurse came over to see me, and said to me these words, "I know you've had a great loss. I know you are suffering right now, and you are trusting for a miracle." I was not waiting for a miracle. I already knew my mother was in heaven, so I'm not sure what this nurse was talking about. She got my attention, and as I listened to her, I could not believe what I was hearing. This nurse was saying that with a charm that she had, she could bring my mother back to life - all I had to do was believe that she could do it.

Wow! Imagine that! The Bible teaches me that only God can give life and take it away. My husband and my sister were all in shock at what this woman was doing. It got to the point that I was looking at her in a state of dismay. What a moment I was living in! I had just said goodbye to someone that was so dear to my life, and my friend, only to hear the unbelievable craziness of what this woman was saying! Let me tell you, she was for real. This woman was speaking things that were so unnatural, just to get me to denounce God. This would have totally made my mother scream! She finally gave up, because I kept ignoring her, and she left. Talk about amazing experiences, this was one for the history books that I will never forget.

Well from that moment on, I realized my father was in heaven, and then my mother went to join him. Now, the enemy was making me feel like I was an orphan, with no one to pray over me. You see, my mother was a prayer warrior, and I knew this. As I prayed and sought the guidance of God, I realized my family was victorious! They won the battle, and they are in heaven. I started thinking, now I have my family's baton. It has been handed to me to continue to run the race that my generation has been running. I pray every day that I can make my God proud.

I am still continuing the race, and you know God is on my side. You often wonder what life would've been like if none of this would have happened. I don't think about that anymore. I am just looking forward, and not looking back anymore. We have been blessed by God in so many ways. God has granted me the ability to become an ordained minister. We have had so many awesome meetings, with so many people turned back to God, and saved. We have had so many events, and he has also paid for all the meetings that I have had, as long as I put him first. I guess that would be another book about all the wonderful things he has done for others, and miracle after miracle.

The ministry is now stronger and we have become greater in God. As we continue in unity, Ephesians 4 is helping others. I must say that after all this battle, God granted me, or rather gave me, the most beautiful gift I could ever imagine. My younger son got married. They now have a beautiful, baby boy who is truly a blessing, and a gift from God.

I will continue to work and do what God called me to do, never looking back but looking forward. I have been truly blessed in all my trials and circumstances, because somehow God has come through and to him be all the honor and glory. He is and will always be my source of strength.

ABOUT THE AUTHOR

Pastor Norma Arce is obeying God's calling. She started in full time ministry in June 2003. Norma is founder of Unity of the Faith, Inc., a ministry located in Palm Beach County, Florida. She teaches and pastors leaders, creating leadership for the Kingdom.

She has helped start two churches, ordained several pastors and set evangelists into position in ministry. She has ministered throughout Florida, and is ordained through World Ministry Fellowship in Plano, Texas. She has two sons and one grandson.